Starving the Anger Gremlin

of related interest

How to Be Angry
An Assertive Anger Expression Group Guide for Kids and Teens
Signe Whitson
Foreword by Dr Nicholas J. Long
ISBN 978 1 84905 867 4
eISBN 978 0 85700 457 4

Little Volcanoes
Helping Young Children and Their Parents to Deal with Anger
Warwick Pudney and Éliane Whitehouse
ISBN 978 1 84905 217 7
eISBN 978 0 85700 595 3

Anger Management Games for Children
Deborah M. Plummer
Illustrated by Jane Serrurier
ISBN 978 1 84310 628 9
eISBN 978 1 84642 775 6

Working with Anger and Young People
Nick Luxmoore
ISBN 978 1 84310 466 7
eISBN 978 1 84642 538 7

STARVING THE Anger Gremlin

A COGNITIVE BEHAVIOURAL THERAPY WORKBOOK
ON ANGER MANAGEMENT FOR YOUNG PEOPLE

Kate Collins-Donnelly

Jessica Kingsley *Publishers*
London and Philadelphia

This edition published in 2012
by Jessica Kingsley Publishers
73 Collier Street
London N1 9BE, UK
and
400 Market Street, Suite 400
Philadelphia, PA 19106, USA

www.jkp.com

30

First published in 2007 by Trafford Publishing

Library of Congress Cataloging in Publication Data
Collins-Donnelly, Kate.
Starving the anger gremlin : a cognitive behavioural therapy workbook on anger management for young people / Kate Collins-Donnelly.
p. cm.
ISBN 978-1-84905-286-3 (alk. paper)
1. Anger--Juvenile literature. 2. Anger in children--Juvenile literature.
3. Cognitive therapy for children--Juvenile literature. I. Title.
BF723.A4C65 2012
152.4'7--dc23
2011048662

British Library Cataloguing in Publication Data
A CIP catalogue record for this book is available from the British Library

ISBN 978 1 84905 286 3
eISBN 978 0 85700 621 9

Printed and bound in the UK by Bell and Bain Ltd, Glasgow

MIX
Paper | Supporting responsible forestry
FSC® C007785

The authorized representative in the EEA is Hachette Ireland,
8 Castlecourt Centre, Dublin 15, D15 XTP3, Ireland (email: info@hbgi.ie)

Contents

Acknowledgements

Thank you to the colleagues that have dedicated their time, positivity, comments and support to this project. A special thank you goes to Maria for her advice, knowledge and unwavering support, as well as her absolute belief in what I was trying to achieve through this book. And last, but by no means least, I would like to thank all the young people who I have worked with and learnt from, especially those who were brave enough to share their stories in order to help others.

About the Author

Hi! I'm Kate, and I provide support for children and young people with emotional difficulties through counselling, coaching and training sessions. I also work with parents and professionals to help them learn how to teach emotional management skills to young people.

The need for a book on anger management aimed at young people became evident through this work. This book is about empowering young people to help themselves by learning about the basics of anger and how to control it.

Some of the young people that I have worked with have kindly contributed their stories, thoughts and drawings to this book in order to help others learn how to control their anger like they have.

In a nutshell, I want to spread the word far and wide on how to manage your anger, but in a simple, activity-filled, easily readable and interesting way. I hope my book achieves this. I'll let you be the judge.

Happy reading!

Kate

Information for Parents and Professionals

The purpose of this workbook

Starving the Anger Gremlin provides a cognitive behavioural approach to anger management for young people. It is designed for young people to work through on their own or with the support of a parent or a professional, such as a teacher, mentor, teaching assistant or youth worker. The self-help materials included in this workbook are based on the principles of cognitive behavioural therapy (CBT), but do not constitute a session by session therapeutic programme. However, the materials contained in this workbook can be used as a resource for therapists working with young people.

What is cognitive behavioural therapy?

CBT is an evidence-based, skills-based, structured form of psychotherapy that has emerged from the work of cognitive therapists such as Aaron Beck and behaviourists such as Pavlov and Skinner. CBT looks at the relationships between our thoughts (cognition), our feelings (emotions) and our actions (behaviours). It is based on the premise that how we interpret experiences and situations has a profound effect on our behaviours and emotions.

CBT focuses on:

- the problems that the client is experiencing in the here and now
- why the problems are occurring
- what strategies the client can use in order to address the problems.

The therapeutic process achieves this by empowering the client to identify:

- negative, unhealthy and unrealistic patterns of thoughts, perspectives and beliefs
- maladaptive and unhealthy patterns of behaviour
- the links between the problems the client is facing and these patterns of thoughts and behaviours
- how to challenge the existing patterns of thoughts and behaviours and implement alternative thoughts and behaviours that are constructive, healthy and realistic in order to address problems, manage emotions and improve wellbeing.

Thus, the underlying ethos of CBT is that by addressing unhelpful patterns of thoughts and behaviours, a person can change how they feel, how they view themselves, how they interact with others and how they approach life in general – thereby moving from an unhealthy cycle of reactions to a healthy one.

CBT has been found to be effective with a wide range of emotional wellbeing and mental health issues, and the National Institute for Clinical Excellence (NICE) recommends the use of CBT for a number of conditions. Although there have been fewer research studies conducted on the use of CBT with children and young people than there have been with adults, evidence for its effectiveness with children and young people is continuing to mount.

Introduction

Do you frequently feel angry?

Do you find yourself hitting, punching, kicking, screaming or damaging things when you get angry?

Do you feel like you have no control over how you feel and how you react when you get angry?

If you answered 'Yes' to any of the above, this book is here to help you!

Starving the Anger Gremlin contains information and activities, as well as comments from other young people, which will help you to control your anger and express it in more positive ways. It really is possible once you learn more about why we get angry and what strategies can help when we do.

The anger management techniques that you will learn as you progress through this workbook have been adapted from the basic principles of something called cognitive behavioural therapy (CBT). CBT is where a therapist helps people to deal with a wide range of emotional problems, including problematic anger, by looking at the links between how we think (our cognition), how we feel (our emotions) and how we act (our behaviours).

This workbook will help you to understand the links between how you think, how you feel and how you act in order to help you manage your anger and get control back!

But remember...

Starting to explore your anger may well raise some really difficult issues for you, so it's important that you can talk to someone you trust about these issues, such as a parent, relative, friend, teacher or counsellor. Part of getting control back is being able to share how you feel with someone else.

1

What is Anger?

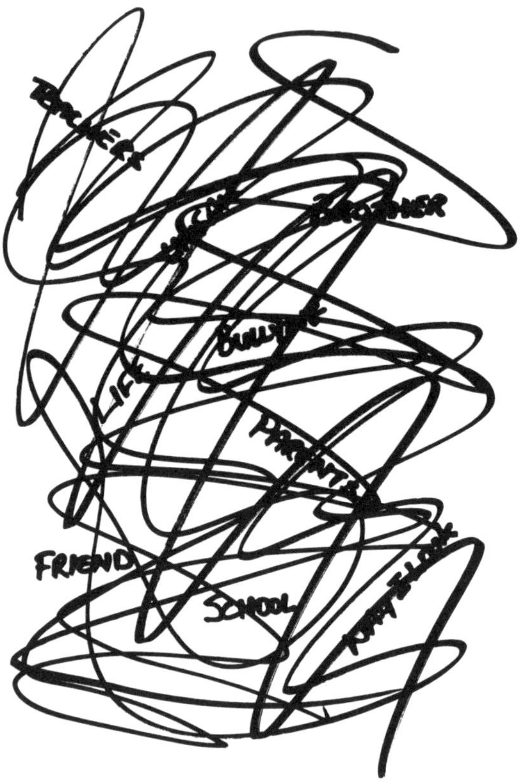

My Anger!
(Tess, 14)

Anger is an important emotion that is normal and natural when used with control. We all get angry.

Anger helps us to cope with:

- threats
- hurt (e.g. if our rights are being violated)
- frustration (e.g. if we feel our basic needs aren't being met).

So anger can be positive if expressed in the right way.

However, anger becomes a problem if it is:

- displayed too frequently
- interfering with aspects of your life (e.g. relationships, school or work)

- used as a tool to get what you want (e.g. if a child realises that he gets attention from his mum when he throws a tantrum)
- displayed aggressively (e.g. fighting, shouting or threatening)
- turned against yourself
- buried inside and bottled up
- taken out on someone else.

Here are some quotes from other young people about their problematic angry behaviours:

'I get into fights when I get angry.' (James, 14)	'I slam doors.' (Will, 15)
'I scream, swear and shout at my mum.' (Pete, 13)	'I hit and kick my brother.' (Carl, 14)
'I throw things and knock things over.' (Molly, 15)	'I say nasty things and shout.' (Phillipa, 12)
'I take it out on myself.' (Emma, 17)	'I smash up the place and put holes in walls.' (Chris, 16)

'I lose it and take it out on my mum. I'm horrible. I punch her.' (Sally, 13)

Do any of these sound familiar?

Don't worry if they do. By understanding more about your anger and by learning how to manage it and express it constructively, your experiences of anger can become more positive!

2

My Anger

Let's start exploring your anger using the My Anger Questionnaire.

MY ANGER QUESTIONNAIRE

1. How often do you get angry? Circle your answer.

a) Often b) Sometimes c) Rarely d) Never

2. Think about how you tend to feel physically when you get angry. Circle any of the following feelings that apply to you.

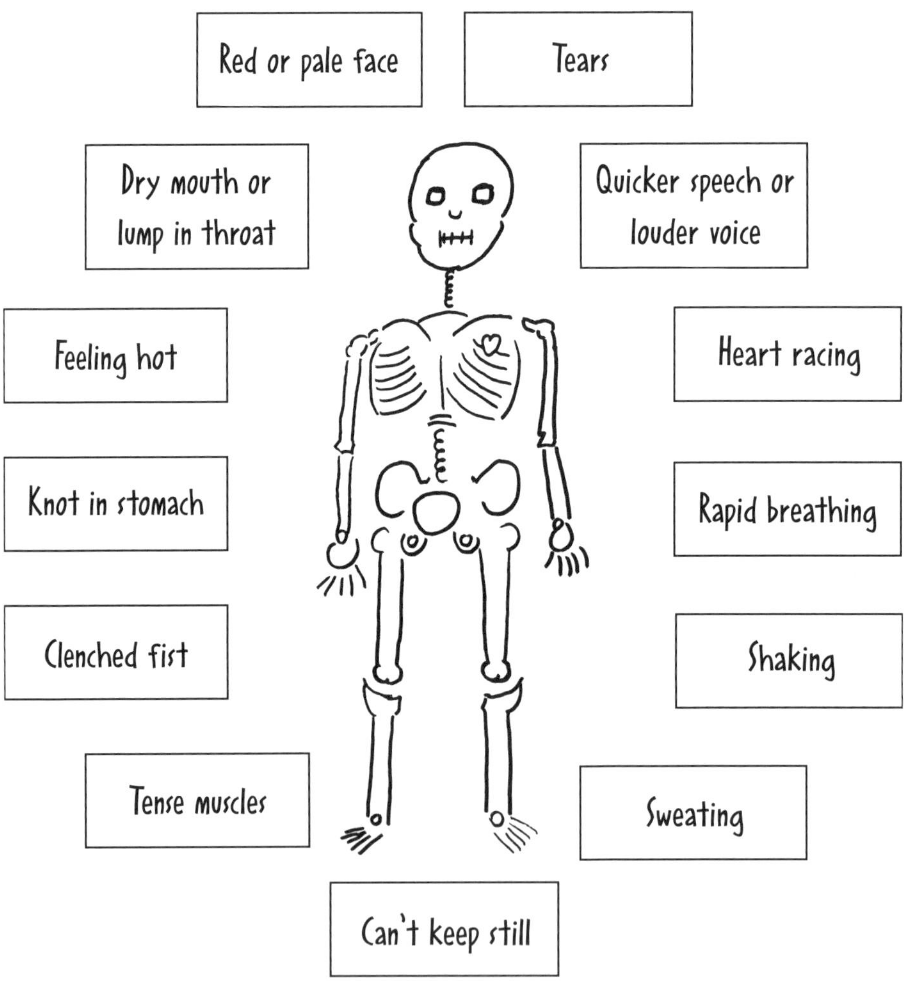

3. Below are different ways that people can react when they get angry. Tick any behaviours from both groups A and B that apply to you when you get angry.

Group A behaviours

- ☐ Threaten
- ☐ Shout
- ☐ Slam doors
- ☐ Criticise myself
- ☐ Punch
- ☐ Swear
- ☐ Make sly digs
- ☐ Kick
- ☐ Bully
- ☐ Start vicious rumours
- ☐ Get revenge
- ☐ Hurt myself
- ☐ Throw a tantrum
- ☐ Snap at people
- ☐ Shove
- ☐ Accuse or blame
- ☐ Throw things
- ☐ Verbally abuse
- ☐ Break things
- ☐ Cry
- ☐ Lose control
- ☐ Get angry with self
- ☐ Bottle anger up
- ☐ Use a weapon
- ☐ Become cold
- ☐ Behave recklessly
- ☐ Give silent treatment
- ☐ Say nasty things
- ☐ Other . . . .

Group B behaviours

- ☐ Talk to someone
- ☐ Calm myself down
- ☐ Count to ten
- ☐ Ignore it
- ☐ Distract myself
- ☐ Walk away
- ☐ Write down feelings
- ☐ Other...............

4. Think about your answers to the previous questions and then rate your anger on the following scale.

1 2 3 4 5 6 7 8 9 10

Not problematic Quite problematic Problematic

Problematic anger

If you have scored your anger as problematic on the scale in Question 4 it's probably because you are getting angry a lot and experiencing several physical symptoms when you get angry (we will look at the effects this has on your physical health in Chapter 8). In addition, most of your angry behaviours probably fall into the group A behaviours category in Question 3.

Q. Do you see any other patterns in your angry behaviours?

- Are you particularly *aggressive*? For example, are you frequently throwing things, punching, kicking, verbally abusing or using a weapon?
- Perhaps you *turn it inwards* (direct it at yourself)? Examples of this include self-criticism and self-harming.
- Or do you tend to try and bottle up your anger? This is known as *suppressing* your anger.

- Or perhaps you direct it at other people, instead of those who you feel have triggered your anger? This is known as *displaced* anger. For example, you get angry because your mum has told you that you are grounded, but instead of expressing that anger towards your mum, you choose to shout at your sister.

You have now completed the first step towards managing your anger, namely assessing what you anger tends to be like. Now let's look at the next step – understanding why your anger occurs.

3

How Does Anger Occur?

What makes you angry?

List anything that makes you angry in your Anger Box below.

ANGER BOX!

What makes me angry?

Your list may include:

- People (e.g. brother)
- Pets
- Places (e.g. school)
- Situations/events (e.g. the arguments between your parents)
- Someone's actions (e.g. your mum telling you off)
- Someone's attitude (e.g. a person's racist attitude)

These are all examples of the things that people list when asked what makes them angry.

However, these only *trigger* an angry reaction. They do not *cause* it.

Let's see what we mean by thinking about the following questions.

Q. You get angry when your PE teacher doesn't pick you for the school team. Is your teacher controlling your anger?

Yes No

Q. If your answer is 'Yes', does that mean she has an anger remote control that she is pointing at you?

Yes No

Q. Is she pressing a big ANGER button that is causing you to get angry?

Yes No

The answer to all three questions is actually 'No'! Your teacher *isn't* pressing an anger button on a remote control to make you angry. She isn't controlling your anger at all.

Q. So who *is* in control of your anger?

You The children who were picked for the team

The answer is you! The remote control is in *your* hands!

It's *your* thoughts and beliefs that make you angry. Anger is about how *you* react to a situation, not the situation itself.

You're the one in control of your anger!

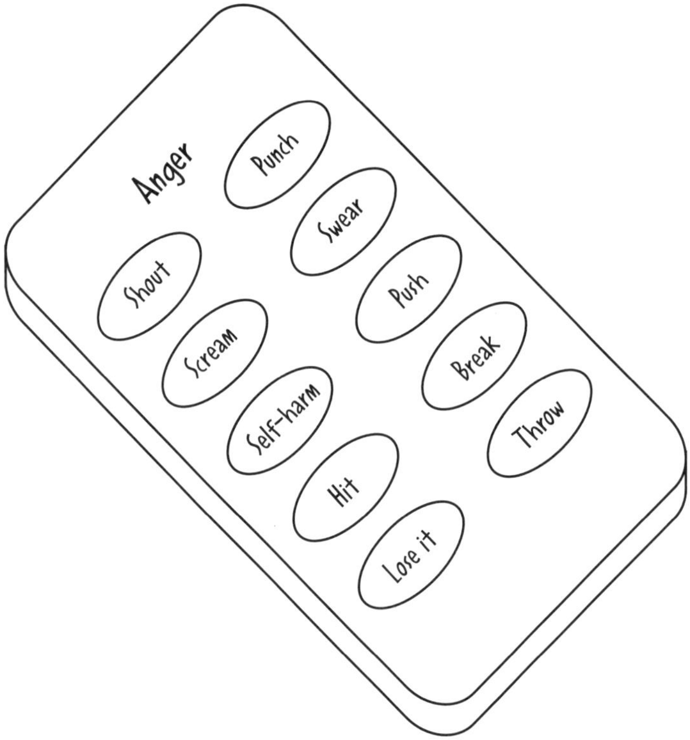

Let's have a look at some examples to see what I mean.

Scenario 1

Your dad is supposed to come to watch you in the school play, but he doesn't turn up. You think to yourself:

'He could've let me know.'

'He's obviously had a better offer.'

'He's probably stuck at work again.'

'I knew he wasn't really interested.'

Q. Rate how angry you think you'd be on the scale below.

1 2 3 4 5 6 7 8 9 10

Not very angry Angry Really angry

OK, now imagine that when you get home you find out that your dad had fallen over, broken his leg and spent the evening at the hospital.

Q. Now how angry would you be on a scale of 1 to 10?

1 2 3 4 5 6 7 8 9 10

Not very angry Angry Really angry

Q. Did you rate your anger as higher or lower than before?

Higher Lower

Let's have a look at another example.

Scenario 2

You work as a shop assistant at weekends and one day the boss asks you to create a display of tinned foods that are on offer. You've just finished balancing the last can when someone crashes into your display and sends the cans flying!

Q. How angry would you be on a scale of 1 to 10?

1 2 3 4 5 6 7 8 9 10

Not very angry Angry Really angry

But let's say the person that has fallen into your display had tripped on something that had been spilt on the floor.

Q. How would you rate your anger now?

1	2	3	4	5	6	7	8	9	10
Not very angry				Angry					Really angry

Q. Did you rate your anger as higher or lower than before?

Higher Lower

I'm sure that in both examples you were less angry in the second version of the story than the first.

Q. So what is it that makes you less angry?

The answer is *you!*

It's not the situation itself that controls your level of anger. If it was, we would all react in the same way in the same situation. However, we don't. Reactions differ from individual to individual.

Q. So if it's not the situation itself that determines your level of anger and type of angry reaction, what is it?

It's how you *think* about the situation.

For example, if you instantly think that the person knocked over your display on purpose, your anger is likely to be greater than if you initially thought that it must have been an accident.

These examples show that you *can* control how you react.

You're the one in control of your anger!

4

Anger Control

So now we've established that you are the one who is in control of how you act when you get angry. But your ability to control your anger at any given point in time can also be affected by other factors. The following task will help you to work out what these factors are. First, read through the different scenarios below.

Scenario 1

Mary is six. Her dad loses his temper all the time and often punches the wall and kicks things. Mary has been getting into a lot of trouble at school recently because when she gets mad or upset over something she hits someone.

Scenario 2

Sam is 16. Whenever Sam wants something he will shout and verbally abuse his parents until he gets it.

Scenario 3

Tim is 13. His parents believe that homosexuality is a sin. Tim finds out that his brother is gay. He loses it and starts a fight with him.

Scenario 4

Sarah is 17. She works three jobs in order to pay her rent and can't afford to take time off. One evening she is on her way home from work and is really tired. Someone bumps into her in the street. She shouts at them and pushes them back.

Scenario 5

Dave is 18. He's just found out that his girlfriend cheated on him with his best mate. That same day Dave is told by his college tutor that his essay wasn't good enough. Dave throws the essay at his tutor, storms out of their office and slams the door.

Now I want you to think about what might be affecting each person's anger control in each of the different scenarios.

See if you can match up the scenario number below with the factor affecting the person's anger control in that scenario.

MATCH THE SCENARIOS

Scenario 1	Beliefs
Scenario 2	External factors, such as relationships, work or school
Scenario 3	Past experiences of how others have expressed and controlled their anger
Scenario 4	Individual differences, such as being hungry, tired, ill or stressed
Scenario 5	Past experiences of how the young person's anger has been responded to

You will find the answers to this Match the Scenarios task in the Appendix.

As you can see, a person can develop a habit of reacting in a certain way when they get angry because of their *past experiences*. We learn from what we see and experience. So we learn from how we see other people acting when they get angry, and from how other people respond to our own angry outbursts.

How a person tends to react can also change depending upon the particular *individual* and *external circumstances* at that point in time, such as being ill or tired, or having experienced a relationship break-up.

But although these things impact on our anger control, they *don't* stop us from being in control of our anger. We cannot use them as excuses.

We are still in control of how we react.

So even when we have a right to be angry (for example, if we are being bullied at school) we cannot react in negative ways, such as taking our anger out on someone else. We need to deal with our anger constructively.

The next step to achieving this improved anger control is to understand the interaction between *the trigger situation* and *your angry reaction* in more detail.

5

The Anger Gremlin

The Anger Gremlin Model

Hungry Trigger → **Feeding** Thoughts and beliefs → **Full** Angry reaction

Think of your anger as a hungry Gremlin sat on your shoulder.

TRIGGER

Now think back to Scenario 1 in Chapter 3, when your dad didn't turn up to your school play. That's the trigger situation – the Anger Gremlin is hungry.

FEEDING

As the model shows, the next stage is 'feeding'. If you immediately begin to think negatively or irrationally about this anger trigger, such as 'He doesn't care about me' or 'I knew he didn't want to come anyway,' you are feeding the hungry Gremlin.

The more you think negatively, the more you feed your Gremlin!

FULL

The bigger and fuller your Anger Gremlin gets, *the angrier you get!*

The Anger Gremlin Cycle

The interaction between the trigger situation and your angry reaction is even more complex than this. Let's look at the complete Anger Gremlin Cycle now.

This cycle shows the links between our thoughts, feelings and behaviours, and is based on a cognitive behavioural approach.

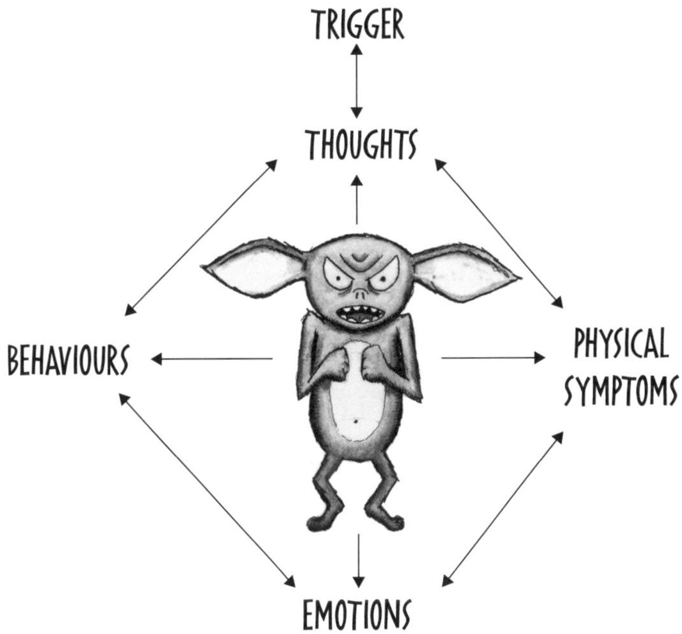

TRIGGER

First you have the trigger situation. Let's use the example of your mum not letting you go out with your friends.

THOUGHTS

Perhaps you begin to think negatively, such as:

'What gives her the right?'

'I deserve to go out!'

'How dare she?'

So you begin to feed the Anger Gremlin.

PHYSICAL SYMPTOMS

Physically you might feel hot and your heart might beat faster as you begin to get angry.

This feeds the Anger Gremlin even more!

EMOTIONS

As a result of these physical feelings your thoughts can become even angrier and more negative.

This can then lead you to feel even angrier emotionally.

So a vicious cycle develops in which the Anger Gremlin is getting bigger and bigger and fuller and fuller!

And you're getting angrier and angrier!

BEHAVIOURS

And the bigger and fuller your Gremlin gets, the more and more problematic your angry behaviours become, and you may react by shouting, swearing or hitting things.

THE CYCLE

The more this vicious cycle develops, the more likely you are to react in the same way the next time the same trigger comes along.

And the more you react negatively to a specific trigger, the more likely you are to react negatively when something else triggers your anger!

So before long you have developed a *habit* of reacting negatively whenever you get angry about anything.

The Gremlin

Think about how your Gremlin might look.

Use the box on the next page or your own piece of paper to draw your Anger Gremlin. Then give it a name!

ANGER BOX!

My Anger Gremlin named

....

6

Starving the Anger Gremlin

Q. Now you've learnt about the Anger Gremlin, how do you get rid of it?

You starve it!

If you don't starve your Gremlin, your anger will continue to become more and more problematic.

You can starve your Gremlin by using different techniques to control your anger and to express it in the right ways. See how many different techniques you can come up with.

ANGER BOX!

Ways to starve my Gremlin

I hope you've come up with a number of different ways. Let's have a look at what you might have included. The techniques discussed here are based on a cognitive behavioural approach.

1. Anger distractions

There are some very basic things that you can do when you feel yourself beginning to get angry, which will help you to ignore your anger and starve the Anger Gremlin. You can:

Do something else instead

Count to ten

Use your trigger word

Walk away

Take deep breaths

Ignore it

Imagine something funny

Think happy thoughts

Anger distractions can work well in some situations. For example, you could come up with a 'trigger word' that lets other people know that you're angry so they leave you to calm down. Saying the trigger word out loud will also make you stop and think before you act. For example, Sally, aged 15, uses 'banana' as her trigger word.

2. Think!

Distractions aren't the only answer. Remember that it's how you *think* about a situation that causes your anger to escalate, not the situation itself. So when you're thinking *negatively* or *irrationally* about a situation you're *feeding your Gremlin!*

Therefore, another way to control your anger is to *think differently!* When you begin to get angry, ask yourself:

Question and challenge yourself in this way, talk to yourself using more positive thoughts and think *before* you act!

The more you do this, the more you'll *starve your Gremlin!* And the more you starve it, the less problematic your angry reactions will be.

3. Challenging your negative thoughts

To learn how we can challenge our negative thoughts, have a look at the example below.

Scenario 1

Emily sends her best friend Jade a text asking her if she wants to come over. Jade doesn't reply.

Q. What *negative* thoughts might Emily be thinking?

ANGER BOX!

Emily's negative thoughts

I've asked many different young people this question while working with them and their anger. Here are some of the answers they've given:

Q. What *more realistic* thoughts could Emily have used instead?

ANGER BOX!

More realistic thoughts

How about these?

Q. Compare the two different sets of thoughts... Which *feed* the Anger Gremlin and which *starve* it?

The first set of thoughts feed the Anger Gremlin. The second set starve it.

Q. Why is this?

Think about the scenario rationally and realistically. Emily didn't get a reply to one text. One text only! It's far more likely that Jade didn't get the message for some reason than that she no longer wants to be Emily's best friend!

Whenever you begin to get angry about something try to think about the situation *rationally* and *realistically* based upon the facts. Make sure you are not blowing the situation out of proportion in your thoughts. Asking yourself the questions on the following worksheet can help you to do this.

ALTERNATIVE THOUGHTS

What situation am I getting angry about?

. . . .

How am I currently thinking about the situation?

. . . .

What are the facts about the situation?

. . . .

Are my current thoughts realistic and rational?

. . . .

How could I think more realistically and rationally in order to starve my Gremlin?

. . . .

4. Constructive reactions

The other thing to think about when you begin to feel yourself getting angry is, 'How should I react?'

Ask yourself, 'If I react in a certain way will I be *feeding* or *starving* my Gremlin?'

There are obviously going to be situations where you feel you have a right to be angry. In these circumstances it is good to express your anger and not bottle it up, but you need to express it constructively.

Let's have a look at a couple of example scenarios to see what I mean.

Scenario 1

Lauren finds out that her boyfriend has cheated on her with two of her mates. She is devastated and incredibly angry. She confronts her boyfriend aggressively, shouting at him and hitting him.

Q. Was Lauren feeding or starving her Gremlin?

Feeding Starving

The answer is feeding!

Q. How could Lauren have expressed her anger in a more positive way to starve her Gremlin?

ANGER BOX!

How could Lauren have starved her Gremlin?

Examples that other young people have given include:

Calmly told him how she feels.

Ignored him.

Asked her mates why they did it.

Calmly told him that he was dumped.

Talked to her mum or to one of her other friends about how she felt.

Talked to him about it when she felt calmer.

Asked him why he did it.

Scenario 2

Chris is late home one evening as the bus had broken down. However, his mum immediately assumes that he had been up to no good. Chris gets angry at being misjudged and loses his temper.

Q. Is Chris feeding or starving his Gremlin?

Feeding Starving

The answer is feeding!

Q. What could Chris have done instead to starve his Gremlin?

ANGER BOX!

How could Chris have starved his Gremlin?

Examples that other young people have given include:

Explained to his mum what actually happened.

Asked his mum for an apology.

Stayed calm.

Got his mum to check with the bus company.

Waited until his mum had calmed down before he spoke to her.

Told her how he felt.

Talked to her.

Scenario 3

Harry's dad died two years ago. He's at school one day and another boy makes a nasty remark about his dad. Harry gets into a fight with the boy. It is broken up by a teacher and Harry gets suspended for starting the fight.

Q. Was Harry feeding or starving his Gremlin?

Feeding Starving

The answer is feeding!

Q. What could Harry have done instead to starve his Gremlin?

ANGER BOX!

How could Harry have starved his Gremlin?

Examples that other young people have given include:

There are two themes that run through all these answers:

1. Talk!
2. Keep calm!

One of the best things that you can do when you feel angry is talk to someone about it!

You can talk to *the person that you are angry with*, telling them how you feel and discussing how things can be resolved. But you need to do this *calmly!* You can use the anger distractions and/or the thinking techniques we've already talked about to help you keep calm.

Also remember that your aim is to talk about how you feel and resolve any issues, not to vent grudges or say upsetting things. Make sure you listen to the other person and show them respect.

You can also talk to *another person that you trust* and feel comfortable off-loading to, such as a friend, parent, relative, teacher, mentor or counsellor. Tell them as calmly as you can about what has happened and how you're feeling. Getting it all off your chest like this can help to put things into perspective and help you to work out solutions to any problems that you may have.

Q. But what happens if there's no one around to talk to?

You can *write your thoughts and feelings down*. Often when you look back over it you will see that things weren't as bad as you first thought they were. To help you get started with this there is an Anger Diary on the following page.

After talking or writing about the situation and your feelings, the next step is to learn from them and to move on!

ANGER DIARY

Date

. . . .

I got angry today because...

. . . .

How I reacted

. . . .

What were the consquences?

. . . .

Did I...

- ☐ Starve the Anger Gremlin – yipee!
- ☐ Feed the Anger Gremlin – boo!

If I fed him, what could I have done differently that would have starved him?

. . . .

Would the consequences have been better?

. . . .

7

Anger Dos and Don'ts!

Now it's time for you to think about everything we've gone through so far. Think about all the negative ways and all the constructive ways of reacting to a trigger situation. From these, I want you to come up with your own list of Anger Dos and Don'ts. Try and come up with at least ten of each!

Some people find it helpful to carry this around with them in their bag or to put it up on their wall at home so that they can look at it and remind themselves what to do at times when they're finding it difficult to control their anger.

ANGER BOX!

Dos	Don'ts

8

Effects of Anger

Now we've looked at both the negative *and* positive ways that you can react when you get angry, i.e. how you can feed and starve your Anger Gremlin.

Q. Do you think that feeding your Gremlin and starving your Gremlin produce different results?

Yes No

Let's start to think about the answer to this by looking at the effects that *feeding* your Anger Gremlin can have on you.

Effects of anger on you

Think about some of the times when you have been angry and fed your Anger Gremlin. Write down how you think feeding your Gremlin has affected you in the Anger Box below.

ANGER BOX!
Effects on me

Here are some stories from other young people about how their anger has affected them:

'My mum doesn't want to spend any time with me any more because of how I've been behaving. She says I'm horrible.' (Gem, 14)

'I'm always in trouble at school.' (Jane, 14)

'My anger confuses me.' (Dan, 13)

'My anger makes me sad.' (Keeley, 13)

'I've got in bother with the police.' (Craig, 16)

'I have to work so hard now to get people to believe in me because I used to be so angry and in trouble all the time.' (Emma, 18)

'I hate who I am. I can't control my anger.' (Christine, 15)

'I self-harm. I don't know what else to do.' (Jen, 17)

'My anger's got me excluded.' (Theo, 16)

'I lost my best friend because I'm so angry.' (Jess, 18)

'I get angry a lot so when something bad happens I always get the blame, even when it has nothing to do with me.' (Joel, 15)

Effects of anger on others

Continue to think about some of the times when you have been angry and fed your Anger Gremlin, but this time, write down how you think feeding your Gremlin may have affected other people around you.

ANGER BOX!

Effects on others

Here are some stories from other young people about how their anger has affected other people around them:

'I threw something at this idiot in my class the other day. I didn't mean to hit him in his eye, but he was winding me up, you know.' (Will, 14)

'People are afraid of me.' (Jack, 16)

'It makes my mum cry.' (Tara, 15)

'My mum kicked me out. She said she couldn't cope with me any more.' (Melinda, 18)

'My sister avoids me.' (Lisa, 12)

'My dad says he doesn't trust me any more.' (Ray, 17)

'I've noticed that my brother's copying what I do. He's getting really moody.' (Darren, 13)

'I beat my mum up a lot when I was younger. I hurt her really bad once.' (Sarah, 16)

'Dad had to spend 100 pounds on a stereo last week as I smashed the last one when I got mad.' (Cindy, 16)

As you can see from your own story and those of others, anger can have an effect on all aspects of our own lives, as well as on the lives of others.

Here are some of the areas anger can affect and how.

Physical health

As well as all the physical symptoms that you saw on the diagram in Chapter 2, anger can also have other physical effects on your body, such as raising your blood pressure and releasing adrenalin. If you are having frequent and/or long-lasting feelings of anger or angry outbursts it can have a harmful effect on your physical health in the long term. For example, frequent and long-term anger has been linked to:

- headaches
- high blood pressure
- heart attacks
- being run down and susceptible to illnesses
- digestive disorders (e.g. ulcers)
- and much more.

Your angry behaviours can also impact on the health of others. For example, if you hit someone, you could cause them physical injury and pain. Also, if people around you have to deal with your angry outbursts on a regular basis, the stress of dealing with this can affect their physical health.

Emotional health

Frequent and long-term anger has also been linked to emotional issues, such as low self-esteem (how you see yourself and feel about yourself), stress, feeling sad and low or feeling frustrated.

As we have seen, dealing with your frequent angry outbursts and their consequences can also cause the people around you emotional distress, stress, upset, anger and sadness, which can then impact on all aspects of their lives, such as their relationships, work and finances.

Relationships and reputations

The way you react when you get angry can impact on your relationships with many different people, such as your parents, friends, boyfriend or girlfriend and teachers. If your anger is frequently displayed in a negative way, it can cause problems and tensions in these existing relationships, and also hinder the development of close relationships with new people in the future.

If you frequently react in a negative way when you get angry, it can also cause you to develop a problematic reputation. As you've seen from the quotes from other young people, this can have an impact on how much people trust you and believe in you. It can also result in you getting the blame when trouble occurs, even when it's not your fault.

Current and future prospects

Your anger doesn't just affect you in the here and now. It can also have long-term effects if you allow a pattern of anger to develop. Your anger can impact on how you perform at school and on your ability to achieve what you want to achieve in the future, such as being given a good reference, which will help you to get into college or university, getting on a sports team or getting and keeping a job. Frequently displaying your anger in an aggressive way can also lead to criminal punishments, such as imprisonment.

Your anger can also affect your prospects on a more day-to-day level. For example, if you want to go out with your mates for the day, this is less likely to happen if you have an angry outburst the night before, as your parents may ground you. The more you behave negatively, the more likely you are to experience negative consequences, such as punishments from your parents, carers or teachers. Such punishments can include detentions, losing your computer or telephone time, losing your mobile phone credit or pocket money, or being grounded.

As you can see, your anger can affect every aspect of your life and also the lives of the people around you.

Your anger not only affects you in the here and now but also in the future.

Now go back to your list of Anger Dos and Don'ts.

Look at your list of Don'ts and write down the effects you think these would have on you and the people around you. Once completed, do the same for your list of Dos.

ANGER BOX!

Effects of the dos	Effects of the don'ts

In the Anger Box below you will see an example by Mark, aged 13.

ANGER BOX!

Dos

Talk to my mum

Walk away

Count to ten

Go to my room

Write down how I feel

Take deep breaths

Think of my brother being covered in paint when he knocked it off the ladder!

Ignore it

Ask myself, 'Is it worth it?'

Effects

Feel proud of myself

Make my mum and dad happy

Don't get into trouble

Resolve things more easily

Don't hurt anyone

Get a better reputation

Make more friends

Get treated like an adult

Get things I want

Be trusted more

Feel better and in control

It is healthier for me

Don'ts

Shout

Scream

Punch

Kick

Throw things

Swear

Break things

Call people names

Say hurtful things

Slam doors

Fight

Effects

Make myself sad

Make my mum and dad sad and stressed

Hurt other people

Get into trouble

Get things taken off me

Get grounded

Get detentions

Get put on report

Lose friends

Cause my mum and dad money worries because they have to replace everything I break

Q. Do you see any patterns in your list and in Mark's list?

The pattern is:

Negative behaviours feed the Gremlin and lead to negative results!

Positive behaviours starve the Gremlin and lead to positive results!

9

Summing Up!

We've now gone through all the methods you need to get your anger under control. It's now down to you to put them into practice.

Only you can change how you react.
It's YOU that's in control of your anger!
You have all the power!

Let's have a quick recap before we finish.

Write down five things that you have learnt about your anger and how to control it in the Anger Box below.

ANGER BOX!

What I have learnt about my anger and how to control it

THE ANGER QUIZ

Let's test what you've learnt in the Anger Quiz!

1. Sam is 15. He is late getting to school as his mum's car had a flat tyre. His teacher tells him not to be late again. Sam swears at the teacher and kicks a chair.

Who is in control of Sam's anger?

a) Sam b) Sam's teacher c) Sam's mum

2. Name three physical signs of anger.

1. ....
2. ....
3. ....

3. Name three angry behaviours.

1. ....
2. ....
3. ....

4. Which of the following can affect your anger control?

a) Your past experiences of how other people react when they get angry

b) Stress

c) Your past experiences of how others have reacted to your anger

d) Tiredness

e) All of the above

5. Jane is 14. Her boyfriend has been cheating on her with her best friend Sarah. As soon as she finds out, Jane punches Sarah.

Who is in control of Jane's anger?

a) Jane b) Jane's boyfriend c) Sarah

6. Jason is 21. He used to get suspended from school a lot for getting into fights. Now he gets into rows all the time over silly little things at work.

Name two ways in which Jason's anger might be affecting him.

1. ....

2. ....

7. Beth is 16 and very angry. Yesterday she got into a fight and smashed the window on someone's car. Beth's mum had to miss a day of work to collect Beth from the police station. Beth is being charged with criminal damage. Beth's mum isn't sleeping very well and is snapping at everyone all the time.

Name two ways in which Beth's anger has affected her mum.

1. ....

2. ....

8. What do you need to do to the Anger Gremlin?

a) Feed it b) Starve it

9. Name two ways to control your anger.

1. ....

2. ....

10. Identify one question you should ask yourself when you begin to get angry.

....

11. Name two things that you could do if you want to express your anger positively.

1. ....

2. ....

12. Name two things that you *shouldn't* do if you want to express your anger positively.

1. ....

2. ....

13. Who is in control of your anger?

a) Something b) Someone else c) You

Turn to the Appendix to see how you've got on!

Well done! I'm sure you did fantastically!

Finally, let's check on what you think your anger is like now. Do you remember the My Anger Questionnaire? Well now I want you to complete the questionnaire again to see how your answers may have changed.

MY ANGER QUESTIONNAIRE

1. How often do you get angry? Circle your answer.

a) Often b) Sometimes c) Rarely d) Never

2. Think about how you tend to feel physically when you get angry. Circle any of the following feelings that apply to you.

Red or pale face

Tears

Dry mouth or lump in throat

Quicker speech or louder voice

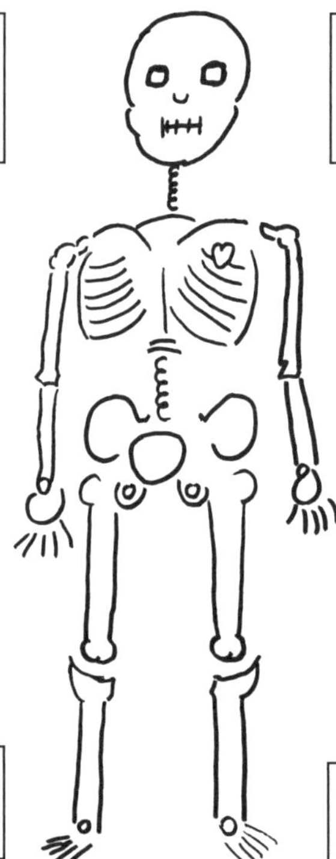

Feeling hot

Heart racing

Knot in stomach

Rapid breathing

Clenched fist

Shaking

Tense muscles

Sweating

Can't keep still

3. Below are different ways that people can react when they get angry. Tick any behaviours from both groups A and B that apply to you when you get angry.

Group A behaviours

- ☐ Threaten
- ☐ Shout
- ☐ Slam doors
- ☐ Criticise myself
- ☐ Punch
- ☐ Swear
- ☐ Make sly digs
- ☐ Kick
- ☐ Bully
- ☐ Start vicious rumours
- ☐ Get revenge
- ☐ Hurt myself
- ☐ Throw a tantrum
- ☐ Snap at people
- ☐ Shove
- ☐ Accuse or blame
- ☐ Throw things
- ☐ Verbally abuse
- ☐ Break things
- ☐ Cry
- ☐ Lose control
- ☐ Get angry with self
- ☐ Bottle anger up
- ☐ Use a weapon
- ☐ Become cold
- ☐ Behave recklessly
- ☐ Give silent treatment
- ☐ Say nasty things
- ☐ Other. . . . .

Group B behaviours

- ☐ Talk to someone
- ☐ Calm myself down
- ☐ Count to ten
- ☐ Ignore it
- ☐ Distract myself
- ☐ Walk away
- ☐ Write down feelings
- ☐ Other. . . . .

4. Think about your answers to the previous questions and then rate your anger on the following scale.

1 2 3 4 5 6 7 8 9 10

Not problematic   Quite problematic   Problematic

Q. Have you seen any changes in your anger since you completed the My Anger Questionnaire at the start of the book? If so, what changes have you seen?

. . . .

. . . .

. . . .

I hope you've seen that your understanding of your anger has improved, as well as your understanding of how to control it.

As you continue to put everything you have learnt from this book into practice, occasionally ask yourself the questions from the My Anger Questionnaire to monitor how far you've progressed and how well you're starving your Anger Gremlin!

That's it guys. All the tools you need to control your anger and express it in the right ways are in this book. Now all you need to do is put them into practice.

And remember:

You have a right to be angry at times Anger is a normal emotion. But *you're* in control of how you react when you get angry. Positive reactions produce positive results! And negative reactions produce negative results!

You are in control of your anger!
You can control it!

Appendix: Quiz Answers

THE ANGER QUIZ

1. (a) Sam
2. See Chapter 2
3. See Chapter 3
4. (e) All of the above
5. (a) Jane
6. See Chapter 8
7. See Chapter 8
8. (b) Starve it!
9. See Chapter 6
10. See Chapter 6
11. See Chapter 6
12. See Chapter 7
13. (c) You!

MATCH THE SCENARIOS

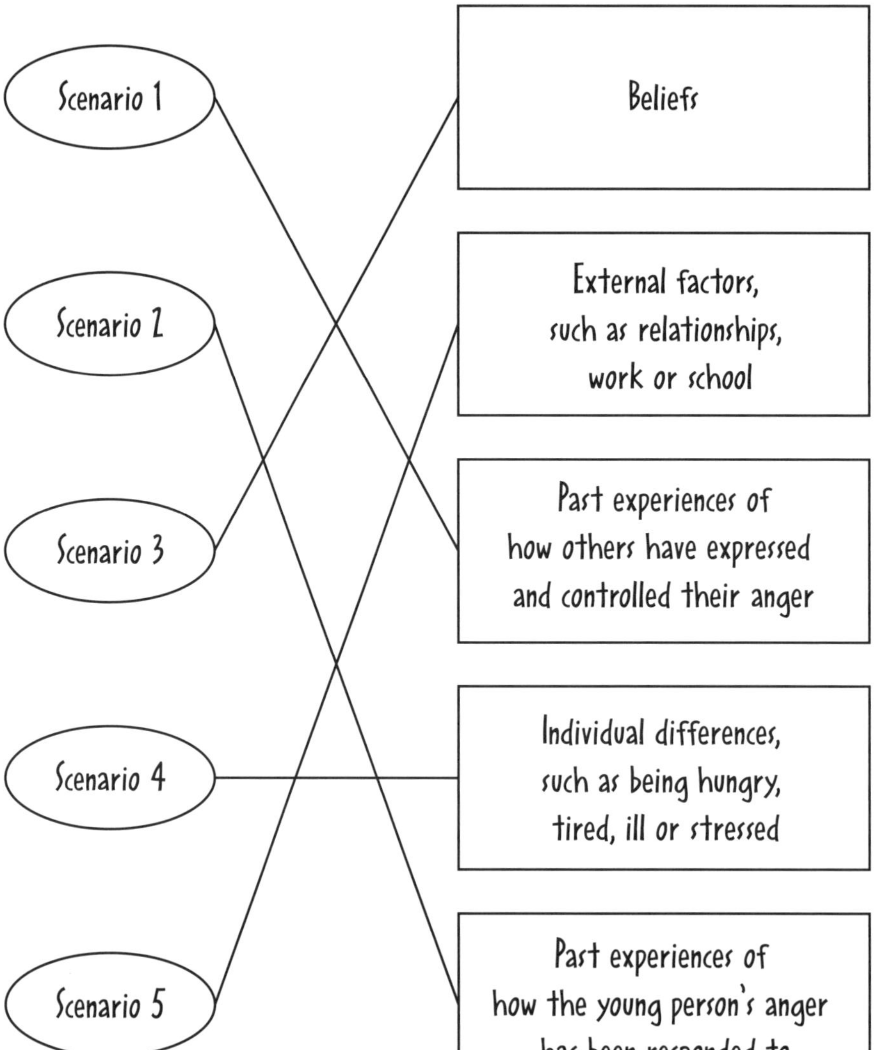

This is to certify that

....

has successfully completed the
Starving the Anger Gremlin workbook
and can expertly

STARVE THEIR ANGER GREMLIN!